HOW TO BECOME A
VENTRILOQUIST

EDGAR BERGEN

Illustrated by
Samuel Nisenson

DOVER PUBLICATIONS, INC.
Mineola, New York

Bibliographical Note

This Dover edition first published in 2000, is an unabridged republication of the work published in 1938 by Grosset & Dunlap, New York. The original illustrations, by Samuel Nisenson, have been retained.

Library of Congress Cataloging-in-Publication Data

Bergen, Edgar, 1903–1978.
  How to become a ventriloquist / Edgar Bergen.
    p. cm.
  Reprint. Originally published: New York : Grosset & Dunlap, 1938.
  ISBN 0-486-41086-2 (pbk.)
    1. Ventriloquism. I. Title.

GV1557 .B4 2000
793.8'9–dc21

                                                    99-054545

Manufactured in the United States of America
Dover Publications, Inc., 31 East 2nd Street, Mineola, N.Y. 11501

CONTENTS

CHAPTER   PAGE

Introduction 9

I Near Ventriloquism 19

II The Doll-Dummy 35

III Hand Puppets 51

IV Shadowgraphs and Cardboard Dummies. 61

V Staging an Entertainment 73

VI Distant Ventriloquism 101

VII Entertaining With Distant Ventriloquism 115

LIST OF ILLUSTRATIONS

PAGE

Edgar Bergen with Charlie McCarthy............Frontis

Ventriloquism was often employed as "black magic".... 11

Positions of tongue and lips when pronouncing vowels.. 21

Charlie is always pert and quick-witted............... 25

Constructing a doll-dummy........................ 37

The mechanics of the dummy's head................. 41

Charlie started his career as a newsboy.............. 47

The hand puppet, Ophelia......................... 55

Some amusing hand puppets........................ 57

A cardboard shadowgraph.......................... 64

Amusing shadowgraphs may be made with the hands
    alone 68

Hold your hands between a bright light and a screen... 69

Rehearse with your dummy before making a public
    appearance 75

These cut-out costumes make a workable Charlie Mc-
    Carthy figure 76

Additional costumes for the Charlie McCarthy figure.. 77

Two-gun McCarthy is a-ridin' the trail!.............. 85

Mortimer Snerd, the country-boy dummy............. 93

Distant ventriloquism requires no dummy........... 105

Your acting ability is important.................... 109

An unseen third person makes a three-sided conversa-
    tion possible 117

Charlie talking from his room upstairs.............. 124

INTRODUCTION

There is no deep, dark mystery about ventriloquism. Anyone, who is willing to practice long and diligently and who possesses a natural flexibility of the vocal cords, can acquire sufficient ventriloquial skill to entertain himself and his friends.

Ventriloquists are not "born," as are successful singers, poets and painters, who must have a definite and inherent ability to sing, write poems and paint. On the other hand, not everyone can become a professionally expert ventriloquist. However, by constant practice, it is possible for the average person to develop a practical skill which will be a source of amusement to himself and others. Also there is always the chance that, while practicing amateur ventriloquy, the student may discover that he has a marked talent for the art which, with more concentrated development, may lead him into the ranks of the professionals.

There are two necessary qualifications for both amateur and professional ventriloquism. First, you must have the determination to practice constantly and regularly because only faithful practice brings the ease and poise which are essential to successful ventriloquy. Secondly, you must possess a natural flexibility of the vocal cords which will permit a variation in the tonal quality and strength of your voice. A third qualification, which is not absolutely necessary but which is of great importance, is a gift of mimicry and dramatic effects. Your success as a ventriloquist will depend a great

Ventriloquism was often employed as "black magic."

deal upon your ability to give the illusion of a human personality other than your own, whether it be an unseen speaker or a puppet.

Ventriloquism is one of the oldest known arts. Historical records show that it has been practiced since the beginning of civilization. In the early centuries it was often employed as an art of "black magic," used by unscrupulous leaders, both religious and political, to frighten and control their superstitious followers. Mysterious voices spoke from the empty air, from the lifeless bodies of idols and from the dark shadows of temples. The listeners, trembling with fear of the unknown, obeyed the commands of these unseen speakers.

Today, of course, ventriloquism is used only as a means of entertainment. The word, ventriloquism, is derived from two Latin words, "venter," meaning the belly, and "loquor," meaning to speak. Thus ventriloquism literally means "speaking from the belly." This, however, is not a correct explanation of the art. The ventriloquist does not speak from his belly. His ventriloquial voice, like his natural voice, originates in the vocal cords in the back of his throat, the changes in tone being created by pressure on the cords. The tighter the cords are stretched, the more rapidly they vibrate and the higher and shriller is the sound which they produce. On the other hand, the more relaxed the vocal cords are, the slower the rate of vibration and the lower the pitch of the sound.

In discussing both amateur and professional ventriloquism, we must always remember that there are two kinds of ventriloquism, the "near" and the "distant." Their names exactly describe them. "Near" ventriloquism requires the use of one or more dummies or puppets and its success depends largely upon the ventriloquist's ability to create the illusion of life in the moving, speaking puppet. It is the type of ventriloquism usually employed by entertainers on the stage, in halls and in private homes. It is the kind which I use with my small, red-headed companion, Charlie McCarthy.

"Distant" ventriloquism requires no dummies or puppets. When this type is used, the ventriloquist's companion is unseen, his voice seeming to come from above or below the ventriloquist or from somewhere in the distance.

It is possible to combine the two forms of ventriloquism, as I shall explain later. But I suggest that, in the beginning, you decide which type you wish to practice and concentrate your efforts on that one kind.

During my ventriloquial career, I have concentrated almost exclusively upon "near" ventriloquism and upon one dummy personality, Charlie McCarthy. When I was a youngster I discovered that my vocal cords possessed a flexibility which made it possible for me to produce voices other than my natural one. I began the study of ventriloquism to amuse and surprise my young friends. It was fun to see the amazement on the faces of the boys and girls when suddenly a strange voice spoke to them.

I practiced many hours, slowly developing ease and smoothness in changing the pressure on my vocal cords and gradually learning to produce a clear and natural-sounding second voice. Then I learned to work with a dummy, which I named Charlie McCarthy. During my school days Charlie and I entertained at parties and in amateur performances and slowly I advanced into the ranks of professional ventriloquists.

During recent years I have developed a few other dummy personalities, but Charlie has been, and is, my most important ventriloquial companion. I use the others for encores for my act with Charlie and they were developed only after many years of experience with one dummy personality.

[15]

HOW TO BECOME A VENTRILOQUIST

In the following pages I shall not attempt to give any instructions or advice in the intricate problems of professional ventriloquism. My purpose in this book is merely to help the amateur to develop a ventriloquial skill for the amusement of himself and his friends.

CHAPTER I

When you listen to little Charlie McCarthy telling me about his adventures and his troubles, you are listening to "near" ventriloquism. By diligent practice you, too, can learn to carry on a conversation with a "Charlie McCarthy" of your own.

The chief difficulty, which the beginner will face in the practice of "near" ventriloquism, is that of keeping his lips motionless while speaking in the voice of the dummy which he is using. Therefore, the first step is to learn to speak clearly and distinctly without moving the muscles of the lips or of the face. You will discover, after careful practice, that this is not so difficult as it may seem.

Stand before a mirror, close your lips until they are from one-eighth to one-quarter of an inch apart, hold your jaws rigid and try to say the five vowels, "A," "E," "I," "O" and "U," without moving your lips. The teeth may touch each other or they may be slightly parted. You will find that you can speak the five vowels clearly and easily without a trace of lip movement.

Next try the consonants. Many letters, "C," "D," "F," which make a sound of the breath striking the teeth but which, if slightly prolonged, have a natural sound without noticeable difference, "G," "H," "J," "K," "L," "N," "Q," "R," "S," "T," "V," which, like "F," must be slightly prolonged, "X," "Y," and "Z," can be easily formed. But the others, "B," "M," "P" and "W," will give you

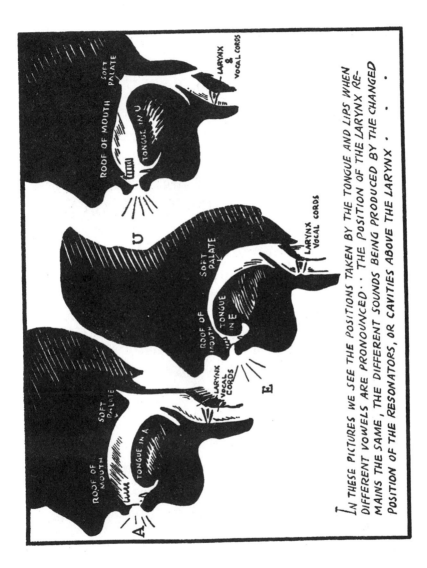

IN THESE PICTURES WE SEE THE POSITIONS TAKEN BY THE TONGUE AND LIPS WHEN DIFFERENT VOWELS ARE PRONOUNCED. THE POSITION OF THE LARYNX RE-MAINS THE SAME, THE DIFFERENT SOUNDS BEING PRODUCED BY THE CHANGED POSITION OF THE RESONATORS, OR CAVITIES ABOVE THE LARYNX.

difficulty. In fact, it is physically impossible to speak them without moving the lips.

Therefore, in arranging the dialogue, which you and your "Charlie" will speak, you must avoid words containing these letters, whenever possible, and substitute other sounds for the difficult consonants when necessary. For instance, the sound, "Vhee," can be used in place of "B" and "Fee" can be substituted for "P." A "big piano" would thus be spoken as a "vig fiano." When used in rapid dialogue these substitutions will not be noticed by your audience.

You must practice the speaking of all the letters with daily regularity, always standing before a mirror, until you can pronounce every letter, or its substitute, without any movement of the lips. When you have finally become expert in speaking without lip movement when you can pronounce the vowels and consonants easily and smoothly and without apparent effort, you are ready for the next step, the study of voice control and change.

The foundation for the ventriloquial voice is the "drone" or "pinched voice." This drone is really a succession of groans or grunts. To produce this voice, hold your teeth together and touch your tongue to the roof of your mouth near the back of your upper front teeth. Take a deep breath and, while holding it, make a groaning sound at the back of the throat, exerting a steady pressure on your vocal cords. As you do this, change the groan into a prolonged "A" or "Ah," exhaling your breath slowly. Repeat this groaned "A" or "Ah," again and again, prolonging the sound as long as possible. You will find that, with constant practice, you will finally produce a clear, humming "A" or "Ah," similar to the sound of a bee's drone. By varying the pressure on your vocal cords, you will discover that you can change the tone of the humming, lowering and raising it as the pressure increases and decreases.

When you have mastered the "drone" with the sound "A" or "Ah," practice droning the other vowels and then the consonants, being very careful to avoid any lip movement. Don't try to hurry through this period of your development. In this practice you are laying the foundation for your ventriloquial voice and for your future success.

The next step is to learn to change rapidly and smoothly from the "drone" voice to your natural voice. Begin by saying "A" or "Ah" in your natural voice, changing quickly to the "drone" or ventriloquial voice. Speak the letter as a clear, sharp, staccato sound in both voices. Practice this rapid change with all the other letters, then with words and, finally, with dialogue sentences. The change from one voice to another must be made smoothly and this skill can be acquired only by constant practice.

Charlie is always pert and quick-witted

When you have mastered a smooth and rapid change from one voice to the other, prepare a short dialogue for yourself and an imagined companion. Stand in front of a mirror and pretend that the unseen second person is standing beside you. Repeat the dialogue again and again, carefully studying your facial expression and absence of lip movement as you speak the words of your invisible friend. Be sure that your face expresses a natural reaction to the speeches of the unseen speaker. The purpose of this practice is to teach you ease in changing voices and dramatic skill in giving the illusion of listening to a second living person. Always remember that you must be a good actor, as well as a skilled ventriloquist, to be successful as an entertainer. Your face and body must express a natural, human reaction to the words of your companion in order to stress the humor or drama of his speeches and to create the illusion of life.

When your mirror tells you that you have mastered the sample dialogue and the change from one voice to the other, you are ready to work with a real doll or dummy. I advise you

to practice first with an imagined dummy, because the manipulation of a real puppet adds another difficulty to your study. When you are using a dummy, you have to consider the movements of its head and body as well as your own facial expressions and voice changes. So I believe that it is wise to go slowly in your practice and to master each step completely, before advancing to the next one.

At this point I want to answer a question which I am asked almost every day. Do I "throw my voice?" The answer is, "No." Pressure on my vocal cords diffuses my voice so that it seems to come from the dummy's mouth, instead of from my own lips. The movements of the dummy's lips complete the illusion. Therefore, it is very important that you practice thoroughly the effective diffusion, or change in pressure, of your ventriloquial voice and the smooth change from one voice to the other, before complicating your efforts by trying to manipulate a dummy.

When you are ready for this next, and very important, step in your progress as a ventriloquist, you must carefully consider the type of doll or dummy with which you are going to work. The selection of your dummy must depend upon the tonal quality and character of your ventriloquial voice. For instance, I discovered that my ventriloquial voice was suited to the personality of a young boy. So I

selected Charlie McCarthy, making him a naughtily whimsical and likeable youngster, with a normal boy's liking for mischief and fun and adventure.

If your ventriloquial voice develops into similar small-boy tones, it will be wise for you to choose a doll with the personality of a youngster, like Charlie. Otherwise, according to the tonal quality, select a little girl, an old man, an old woman or any one of a dozen character personalities, such as a colored man, a farmer or a salty sailor. You have an almost unlimited field of human personalities from which to choose.

Then, when you have made the selection, do your best to develop that doll personality into a real and natural one. It is far better for the amateur to concentrate his attentions and efforts on one doll personality than it is for him to switch from one to another, thus, like the Jack-of-all-trades, becoming really expert with none.

The next step in your study is to learn to coordinate the manipulation of your dummy with the dialogue and your own facial expressions. Stand with your puppet in front of a mirror. Speak a sentence in your natural voice and count the number of times you open and close your mouth. Then speak the same sentence in your ventriloquial voice, moving the puppet's mouth in exact imitation of your own lip movements. By continued practice with

the doll the natural manipulation of its head and lips will become as easy as playing the piano while reading music. Remember that the natural movements of your doll are very important in producing the illusion that your diffused voice is coming from the puppet's mouth. So be very sure that you can manipulate your doll with ease and smoothness before attempting to make a public appearance.

A doll-dummy, like Charlie McCarthy, is not absolutely necessary to the practice of "near" ventriloquism. You can use hand puppets, shadowgraphs and cardboard dummies with almost equal success. In the next chapters I shall explain the use of these various types of puppets.

CHAPTER II

THE DOLL-DUMMY

A doll-like dummy, similar in construction and action to Charlie McCarthy, is probably the most effective help in staging a "near" ventriloquism entertainment. These doll-dummies can be either constructed or purchased. Since the building of a practical doll is a difficult task for a beginner, a ready-made doll will best solve the amateur's problem. You can buy ventriloquists' dolls of all kinds, shapes and sizes in department stores. Then, if the personality of the purchased doll does not fit your ventriloquial voice, you can easily change hair and costume to give the doll the desired appearance.

If you prefer to construct your own doll, you will face an intricate and difficult task. The essential features of a practical doll-dummy are a movable head attached to a hollow neck-stick or pole, a detached jaw, a hollow body into which the neck will fit and well-balanced cords or levers to manipulate the jaw. The entire head will be manipulated by moving the neck-pole. More elaborate dolls also have movable eyes, but this is not necessary as the movement of the head will produce the same effect as rolling eyes.

The most durable and life-like doll-dummy head is one made of wood, similar to Charlie McCarthy's head. Charlie's head was carved eighteen years ago by a Chicago wood-carver. If you are skilled with the wood-carving knives, you, too, can construct an excellent and natural-looking head.

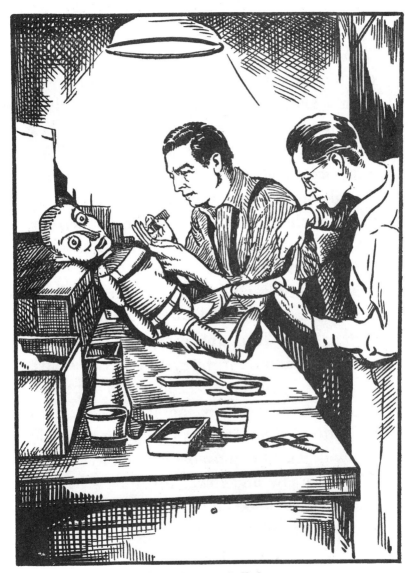

Constructing a doll-dummy

To make such a head, select four pieces of soft pine wood of the dimensions necessary to form a head of the desired size. Glue these four pieces firmly together, forming a box which is hollow and open at both ends. Then construct a smaller box of thinner wood, seven or eight inches long and just large enough to fit inside the head-box. Push the smaller box into the head-box and glue it firmly, thus forming the neck.

Next mark out a face on the chosen side of the head-box and cut the wood away from it, shaping it to form the cheeks and forehead with indentations for the eyes. After you have carved the upper lip, make an oblong opening in the wood below it, extending the opening to the bottom of the piece of wood. In this hole you will place the movable lower jaw. Carve this lower jaw and lower lip from a narrow piece of hard wood and pivot it into the opening by means of a straight piece of wire driven through the face from cheek to cheek. The lower jaw must be constructed to work easily and smoothly on the wire which, after being driven through the face, should be cut off as closely as possible to the cheeks on both sides. Be sure to carve a narrow ridge back of the lips on both the upper and the lower jaws. On this strip the teeth will be painted later.

Attach a small screw ring to the underside of the movable lower jaw and fasten to it a strong string or a piece of flexible picture-wire, long enough to reach down through the hollow neck and into the body. Insert another screw ring in the upper side of the lower jaw, near the back edge. Hook a small spiral spring to this ring and attach the other end to the upper edge of the piece of wood which forms the back of the head. This spring must be strong enough to pull the mouth shut after the lower jaw has been opened by a tug on the string or picture-wire.

When the edges of the head and neck boxes have been rounded, they are ready for painting. The wood should be tinted a natural flesh color with pink cheeks and a red mouth. The teeth may be merely suggested by alternate red and white strips on the ridges back of the lips. The eyebrows should be painted a very dark red or brown or a ruddy-black.

If you wish, you can obtain the eyes from a taxidermist or a doll store and insert them in the indentations left in the face for that purpose. Or you can paint very effective and natural-looking eyes onto the face. A small wig may be used to cover the open end of the head-box. However, if you do not wish to buy a wig, you can use a hat or bonnet, depending, of course, on the sex of the dummy, to cover the open space, painting a suggestion of hair beneath the hat.

If you do not wish to attempt the making of a wooden head, you can mold one from

The mechanics of the dummy's head

plaster of Paris or other plaster compositions or papier mache. Also, if you wish, you can paint the hair onto a molded plaster head, instead of using a wig. However, I believe that you will find that molding a head is an even more difficult task than making one from wood.

The doll-dummy's torso is a box of thin wood or metal with an open back through which the ventriloquist inserts his hand to manipulate the head-pole. To this torso are attached the arms and legs, which may be made of a plaster composition or of cloth, sewed into the proper shapes and stuffed with cotton or excelsior. The hands, if exposed, should be made of tinted plaster. It will probably be much easier for the amateur doll-builder to use small, cotton-stuffed gloves instead of making plaster hands. These gloves can be sewed to the ends of the arms.

The head-pole is inserted into the hollow

body through a round hole in the shoulder piece of the torso-box. To this head-pole are

attached the levers or pull-cords, with finger rings at the ends, which move the dummy's jaw and its eyes, if it has movable eyes. Thus the ventriloquist can move the levers or pull the cords with his fingers, while grasping the pole to manipulate the entire head.

In dressing the doll-dummy, all garments for the upper body must have an opening in the back to permit the insertion of the ventriloquist's hand. The clothes, of course, must be designed to fit the doll's personality. Small shoes, stuffed with cotton and sewed to the ends of the legs, will solve the foot problem.

In elaborately constructed dummies the arms are movable and are manipulated by levers or cords, similar to the ones used for moving the jaw and eyes. But this kind of doll would probably be too difficult for an amateur to construct and manipulate.

My advice is to make your doll as simple as possible. Thus you will avoid difficulties and complications in its manipulation which might mar the effectiveness of your entertainment. Charlie McCarthy is a very simply constructed doll. His jaw is the only movable part of his head and is manipulated by a lever attached to the head-pole. His body is made of thin metal

sheets. His hands are molded plaster, carefully tinted to look like human flesh. His eyes are carved into the head and are painted a dark brown. His head is covered with a wig of reddish-brown.

Charlie's personality has had two phases during his eighteen years of "life." In his early years he was a gay, little newsboy, dressed in sweater and cap. During that time he spoke in the slangy, careless words of a boy who had had to make his own way in the world. Later he "dressed-up," taking on a smoother polish in his clothes and manner of speaking. Today his regular costume is full evening dress, complete with top hat and monocle. But he is fundamentally the same merry, impish Charlie in "tails" that he was when he appeared in sweater and cap.

I advise you to do with your doll-dummy as I have done with Charlie, develop a definite personality and stay with it. First, decide what type of doll fits your ventriloquial voice. Then name the doll and dress it according to the desired personality. Make it real and human,

Charlie started his career as a newsboy

not grotesque and exaggerated. You will find that working with one type of doll, which possesses definite voice and speech characteristics, will hasten your progress in becoming a successful amateur ventriloquist.

CHAPTER III

If you do not wish to buy a doll-dummy or to try to make one, you can use a hand puppet with surprising effectiveness. Its name exactly describes this kind of puppet. The ventriloquist's hand forms the face of the puppet, his thumb and forefinger making the movable mouth.

Often, when I am making public appearances with Charlie McCarthy, I use a hand puppet for an encore. I have named the puppet Ophelia and, as part of the entertainment, I construct her in full view of the audience.

However, I suggest that amateur ventriloquists make their puppets before appearing in front of their audiences.

Making a hand puppet is a far easier task than constructing a doll-dummy. Hold the palm of your right hand toward the ground and double your thumb at the first joint, hiding it under your fingers. Then curve your fingers at the first joints, making a rounded arch. Color the upper part of the thumb and the lower part of the first finger with dark red rouge or paint, forming the lips which will

move when the thumb is moved up and down as the puppet talks. Sketch a nose and eyes with charcoal or black paint on the first finger.

Then snap into place, by means of rubber bands, a hat or cap or small wig to frame the face of the puppet.

When the puppet's head is finished, the next problem is the costume. The clothing will de-

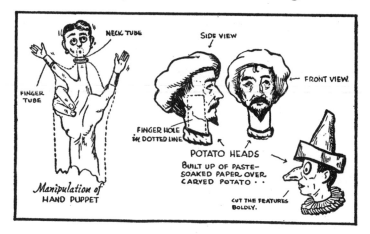

pend, of course, upon the personality of the puppet. With a hand puppet, as well as with a doll-dummy, you must select the type of personality which best fits your ventriloquial voice. The costume can be either a doll's dress, for a woman or girl puppet, or a doll-size suit

The hand puppet, Ophelia

of clothes, stuffed with cotton, for a man or boy. Fasten the garments to your hand with rubber bands to hold them firmly in place. If you wish a very simple costume, a large handkerchief or napkin will serve as a dress.

When using a hand puppet, hold your hand so that the face is level with your own, turning the head from yourself to the audience as the dialogue demands. Carefully practice the movements of your thumb so that you can produce a natural and smooth "lip" movement to fit the puppet's conversation.

Some amusing hand puppets

HOW TO BECOME A VENTRILOQUIST

You will find a hand puppet very amusing and entertaining and very inexpensive to make. When I work with Ophelia, I use a "pinched voice" several tones higher than the voice I use for Charlie McCarthy. However, I do not advise the beginner to experiment with more than one voice. Decide upon one voice and one puppet personality and concentrate your efforts on them alone. Later, after you have had long experience, you can add other puppets and other voices to your collection.

CHAPTER IV

Shadowgraphs offer two advantages to the beginner in ventriloquism. First, they make it possible for him to practice ventriloquism without the expense of a doll-dummy. Secondly, they give him the opportunity to stage an amusing entertainment without revealing his own face to the eyes of his audience, if he is not sure of his ability to speak in his ventriloquial voice without lip movement.

There are two kinds of shadowgraphs, the cardboard cut-out type and the hand shadowgraph. The cardboard cut-out is probably the more effective for amateur entertainment purposes.

To make a cardboard dummy, cut a human face, profile view, from a piece of heavy cardboard. Detach the lower jaw and fasten it to

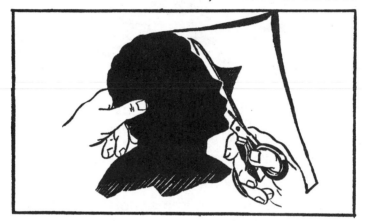

the head by means of wire or small clamps, which will allow it to move freely. Firmly glue a long strip of cardboard or very thin wood to the back of the movable lower jaw, thus forming a hand-piece for the ventriloquist's use in manipulating the dummy's lips and jaw.

It is possible to work with the dummy head, alone. However, if you wish, you can cut out an entire cardboard body, clothed according to the desired sex and personality. If you wish a more elaborate dummy, you can detach the

arms and legs, fastening them to the body by means of wires or clamps and moving them, by means of cardboard or light wood hand-pieces, as you move the lower jaw.

When you and the cardboard dummy are

A cardboard shadowgraph

ready for a public appearance, stretch a small sheet or screen across the end of the room or platform. Place a bright, strong light behind the sheet, focusing its rays on the center of the sheet. The smaller the point of light, the clearer the resulting shadow will be. A large light causes a blurring of the edges of the shadow. The ideal light is a powerful electric bulb with a metal reflector, which will focus the rays onto a small area of the sheet or screen.

When the light and screen are arranged, stand behind the screen and hold the cardboard dummy between the screen and the light, making sure that its shadow falls clearly on the screen and is plainly visible to the audience. With equal effectiveness you can place yourself and the light in front of the screen, or in front of a light-colored or white wall, and hold the dummy between the light and the screen.

If you stand behind the screen, you can speak for the dummy without running the risk of making a tell-tale movement of your own lips. Also, if standing in front of the screen, you can turn your head toward the shadow and away from the audience, thus hiding your own face. Wherever you stand, you must be sure to manipulate the cardboard dummy's mouth and body to accord with the dialogue spoken in your ventriloquial voice.

If you do not wish to work with a cardboard dummy, it is possible to make successful and amusing shadowgraphs by using merely your hands. To do this, form your hands into the shape of a human head, using your fingers to make the movable lips and jaw. Then hold your hands between a bright light and a screen and make the shadow talk. You will find, by experimenting, that it is possible to make many different types of shadow heads and faces. But, again, I suggest that you decide upon one head, whether it be a hand shadowgraph or a cardboard cut-out, and one ventriloquial voice and concentrate on them.

As you grow more expert in making shadowgraphs, you can combine hand and cardboard shadows to form more elaborate

dummies. Your hands will, of course, form the movable parts of the shadow, while cardboard cut-outs will be used to make hats, wigs, bodies, canes, pipes, fans and any other accessories which you may wish.

[67]

Amusing shadowgraphs may be made with the hands alone

· WOLF ·   · GOAT ·   · OX ·

·RABBIT·   ·TEDDY BEAR·   · DOG ·

· DONKEY·   ·BUTTERFLY·

Hold your hands between a bright light and a screen

However, my advice, if you are using a shadowgraph, is to keep your cardboard cut-out or your hand shadow as simple as possible so that you can manipulate it with ease and sureness.

CHAPTER V

After long and regular practice with your doll-dummy, hand puppet or shadowgraph dummy, you will be ready for a public entertainment. Before you appear in front of an audience you must feel within yourself a sureness of your own ability. Complete ease and poise are necessary for a successful act and they can be gained only by the inner knowledge that you are "good."

If possible, arrange your audience's seats at least ten feet away from you. Distance helps to create the illusion of life in your dummy.

[73]

Rehearse your dialogue and action thoroughly before making a public appearance. Always remember that carefully written dialogue, designed to fit the personalities of yourself and your dummy, is as necessary to your success as is your skill in performance. In preparing your dialogue, it is wise to do most of the talking in your natural voice, giving the dummy the smaller share of the conversation.

Also, when writing the dialogue, you can arrange to repeat clearly and plainly in your own voice, the words which contain difficult consonants and which must therefore be slurred in your ventriloquial voice. When they hear your distinct repetition of the dummy's indistinct words, your listeners will not notice the slurring of the puppet's speech. For instance, if your dummy says, "I wish I had a vig fiano," you can reply immediately, "So you wish you had a big piano, do you?"

In using a doll-dummy, place the doll so

Rehearse with your dummy before making a public appearance

MOUTH HOOKS ON TAB AT EAR

KERCHIEF

CATCH TOP OF CHARLIE'S HEAD IN SLIT V FROM THE BACK

HOOK HOLSTER INTO SLITS AT BELT OF TROUSERS

COWBOY SCARF, TIED IN FRONT

SCARF WORN WITH BLACK BERET

BERET

COWBOY SCARF

These cut-out costumes make a workable Charlie McCarthy figure

Additional costumes for the Charlie McCarthy figure

that its head is on a level with your own. Sitting in a chair, with the doll on your knee, will probably give you the greatest ease. Also standing beside a high stool or table, on which the dummy is sitting, may be effective.

Humor, of course, is the most important quality of successful dialogue for any type of ventriloquial entertainment. This humor must accord with the character and personality of the dummy. Don't try to force your comedy. Make it natural and apparently spontaneous.

Speak loudly and clearly in both your natural and ventriloquial voices. Mumbled, indistinct words will spoil your comedy and dramatic effects. Maintain a rapid tempo throughout your act. Never let the conversation drag. Even very clever dialogue, if spoken slowly and haltingly, will fail in its effect.

A song is always a valuable addition to a ventriloquial entertainment. But I do not advise the beginner to attempt to sing. Songs should be added only after you have developed your ventriloquial speaking voice until it has become almost "second-nature" to you. Your

ventriloquial singing voice, when you do use it, must be a tonal outgrowth of your speaking voice, possessing the same fundamental qualities and characteristics of tone. Then it will seem natural for the puppet to burst into song.

In preparing my dialogues with Charlie Mc-

Carthy I always keep in mind that he is a mischievous small boy with great enthusiasm and a keen zest for living and having fun. I try to keep his conversation and the thoughts and actions which he describes in his speeches, in character with his exuberant, boyish personality.

You must follow the same method in writing the dialogue for your puppet, whether it be masculine or feminine, young or old. Treat your dummy as an author treats a character in a book. Make it alive and human, speaking words which fit the definite personality which you are creating.

For instance, the dialogues which I prepare for Charlie McCarthy and for Mortimer Snerd, one of my secondary dummies, are entirely different. I have made Mortimer a slow-witted, shy country bumpkin, who speaks in a low-pitched, twangy drawl. The fundamental quality of his humor is an unwitting dumbness, the exact opposite of Charlie's quick, keen wit. Consequently I prepare their dialogues from two different viewpoints and in two different styles of conversation.

The following is one of the dialogues which Charlie McCarthy and I used on a radio broadcast. You can, if you wish, follow it as a model in writing the dialogue for yourself and your own "Charlie."

* * * *

EDGAR BERGEN: Well, Charlie, you certainly are full of that western spirit tonight. And that's a very becoming cowboy outfit you're wearing.

CHARLIE McCARTHY: I hope to tell ya, pardner. Two-gun McCarthy is a-ridin' the trail. I'm an old cowhide—I mean cowhand.

BERGEN: Now, wait a minute, Charlie. Where did you get that cowboy outfit?

CHARLIE: I bought it, Mr. Bergen. It's my

[81]

reward for many weeks of hard work and savings.

BERGEN: I didn't know you could save money.

CHARLIE: I ran into pay-dirt.

BERGEN: Where did you buy that suit, Charlie?

CHARLIE: In a department store. So help me, that's where I got it.

BERGEN: Hasn't Skinny Dugan a suit just like that?

CHARLIE: Oh—did he?

BERGEN: Are you sure that isn't Skinny's suit?

CHARLIE: Well, you see—I was in the store —the store didn't have my size—so—see? Skinny and I are pals.

BERGEN: Then it is Skinny's suit.

CHARLIE: Well—er—yes. He wanted me to wear it.

BERGEN: Did Skinny say that?

CHARLIE: Well—not exactly. I went over to Skinny's house. Nobody was home and I happened to look in the basement and I saw his cowboy suit hanging on the clothesline.

BERGEN: Yes. Go on, Charlie.

CHARLIE: And I thought, "Somebody might break in and take that suit."

BERGEN: So?

CHARLIE: So I broke in the window and saved the suit.

BERGEN: Then you deliberately took Skinny's suit.

CHARLIE: Well—yes—if you want to put it that way.

BERGEN: The suit looks like a stolen suit, Charlie.

CHARLIE: The hat fits swell. But I must be in the pants too far because the belt buckle scratches my chin.

BERGEN: Have you been out riding?

CHARLIE: What do you think makes me

[83]

walk this way? I went horseback riding. Now I've got that old feeling.

BERGEN: Then you're not much of a horseman, are you, Charlie?

CHARLIE: Oh, yes—I'm quite a horseman.

BERGEN: Well, you haven't convinced me.

CHARLIE: I couldn't convince the horse, either. I went for a moonlight ride last night.

BERGEN: Why did you go at night?

CHARLIE: The man wants a dollar and a half during the day.

BERGEN: How much does he ask at night?

CHARLIE: He's not there at night.

BERGEN: Charlie, you don't mean—

CHARLIE: Don't press me, Mr. Bergen. I was just walking along and, the first thing I knew, I was on a horse.

BERGEN: Yes, Charlie—

CHARLIE: And the next thing I knew, I was off the horse. But I carried on. I wasn't going to let a horse make a fool out of me.

Two-gun McCarthy is a-ridin' the trail!

BERGEN: Oh, no, of course not, Charlie.

CHARLIE: And then away we went—like lightning. Suddenly we came to a fence.

BERGEN: Did you take the hurdle?

CHARLIE: I did—but the horse didn't. That was my first experience in blind flying.

BERGEN: I see.

CHARLIE: I went for half a block before I missed him. I looked down and suddenly he was gone.

BERGEN: Where did he go?

CHARLIE: I don't know. He sort of slipped out from between me.

BERGEN: Any teacher will tell you that a good rider becomes part of the horse.

CHARLIE: What part?

BERGEN: By that I mean that you ride with the horse. When the horse goes up—you go up—and vice versa.

CHARLIE: The trouble was that I went up and the horse went vice versa.

BERGEN: Well, you mustn't argue with the horse, Charlie.

CHARLIE: I was willing to meet him half way—and the most of the time I did.

BERGEN: What kind of a horse did you have, Charlie? A pacer or a trotter?

CHARLIE: He was a bouncer. Did I tell you about Skinny Dugan showing me how to ride and picking up a handkerchief with his teeth?

BERGEN: Did Skinny do that?

CHARLIE: Yes, he did. And then he went back and picked up his teeth.

BERGEN: Ah, but riding is a wonderful sport, Charlie. And it's not especially dangerous if you're careful.

CHARLIE: No matter how careful you are, it will get you in the end.

BERGEN: There's nothing like riding at a dead gallop over hill and dale. It makes you glad that you're alive, doesn't it?

CHARLIE: Glad isn't the word. I'm amazed.

BERGEN: Well, did you get back to the stable safely?

CHARLIE: Yes and no. We came to a fork in the road and the horse gave me an argument.

BERGEN: What do you mean, an argument?

CHARLIE: The horse wanted to go to the right and I wanted to go to the left.

BERGEN: So what happened?

CHARLIE: He tossed me for it. I went his way and he went mine.

BERGEN: Charlie, I think you'd better stop this night riding. What are you trying to be—another Paul Revere?

CHARLIE: Either that or one of the Four Horsemen of the Acropolis.

BERGEN: Charlie—the Acropolis is a ruin!

CHARLIE: Well, that's me. Yippee!

To illustrate the difference in dialogues for various puppet personalities, I am including one of the dialogues which I have prepared for Mortimer Snerd, my country-boy dummy. As you will see, Mortimer's conversation is very

different from Charlie McCarthy's. The shy, bashful and rather dull-witted Mortimer speaks in a nasal, twangy voice and talks more slowly than Charlie. If you have decided to make your own puppet a country-boy type of personality, you can, if you wish, use the following dialogue as a model.

[89]

HOW TO BECOME A VENTRILOQUIST

* * * *

EDGAR BERGEN: You're an interesting young man. What's your name?

MORTIMER: Who? me?

BERGEN: Yes.

MORTIMER: What?

BERGEN: Your name—what is it?

MORTIMER: Mortimer.

BERGEN: What's your last name?

MORTIMER: It's—It's—Gosh!—It's Mortimer.

BERGEN: No. That's your first name.

MORTIMER: Oh—yeah—yeah—so it is.

BERGEN: Don't you know your last name?

MORTIMER: Sure I do. I know it as well as I know my own name. But I can't think of it. Shucks! Ain't that disgustin'?

BERGEN: Why, Mortimer! Surely you know your own last name. What is it?

MORTIMER: Jest a minute. I'm a-workin' on it. Oh—I got it! It's Snerd!

BERGEN: Well! So that's it! Mortimer Snerd!

MORTIMER: Yep. That's me.

BERGEN: Where do you live, Mortimer?

MORTIMER: On the farm.

BERGEN: Is that so? And what are you doing in the city?

MORTIMER: I come to town with a load of pigs. When we was a-loadin' 'em, one of 'em got away. So there was room for me.

BERGEN: Wasn't it rather unpleasant—riding with the pigs?

MORTIMER: Gosh—no. I didn't mind it. They was our pigs. It wasn't like a-ridin' with strangers.

BERGEN: I see. Do you raise anything besides pigs on your farm?

MORTIMER: Sure. Cows. I milk five cows all alone every day.

BERGEN: That's a real job. You're an important man with those cows, aren't you?

MORTIMER: Yep. I'm the main squirt.

BERGEN: Why don't you use an electric machine, Mortimer?

MORTIMER: Shucks! I ain't got no use for them contraptions. They're no good.

BERGEN: Why do you say that? Have you ever tried one?

MORTIMER: Yep. Once. The cow kicked the end of the barn out.

BERGEN: What happened?

MORTIMER: There was a short circuit in the milkin' contraption.

BERGEN: Have you any brothers and sisters, Mortimer?

MORTIMER: Yep. Three brothers.

BERGEN: Where are they?

MORTIMER: One's in the country—itchin' to git to the city. The other's in the city—itchin' to git to the country.

BERGEN: What about the third one?

MORTIMER: Oh—he's a bum. He's just itchin'.

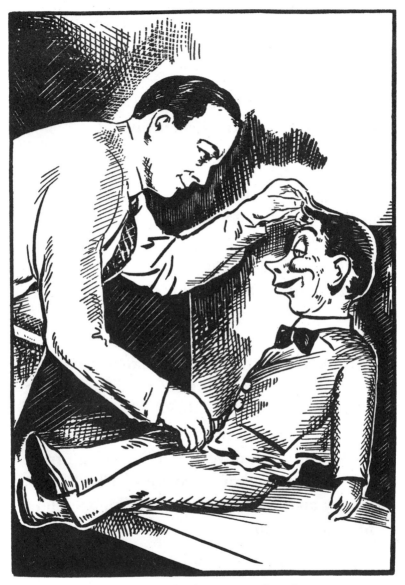

Mortimer Snerd, the country-boy dummy

BERGEN: Well—I'm certainly glad that I met you, Mortimer.

MORTIMER: You're welcome. If you ever come out to the farm, look me up.

BERGEN: I certainly will.

MORTIMER: When do you think you kin come out?

BERGEN: I haven't any idea.

MORTIMER: Is that definite?

BERGEN: Yes, it is.

MORTIMER: Okay. I'll meet you there then. S'long.

Another illustration of the different types of dialogue is the following short dialogue which I have prepared for my hand puppet, Ophelia. Since Ophelia is supposed to be a middle-aged "old maid," her conversation differs both from the crisp, fast-talking repartee of Charlie McCarthy and from the slow, drawling speech of Mortimer Snerd.

* * * *

EDGAR BERGEN: Your name's Ophelia, isn't it?

OPHELIA: Yes, it is.

BERGEN: Are you married, Ophelia?

OPHELIA: No—darn it—no.

BERGEN: Are you thinking of marrying anyone?

OPHELIA: Yes, Mr. Bergen, I am.

BERGEN: Who?

OPHELIA: Anyone. Do you know, Mr. Bergen—a man kissed me once!

BERGEN: Why, Ophelia!

OPHELIA: I guess I am pretty wild, Mr. Bergen. But a girl has to have some fun.

BERGEN: Where did you meet this Romeo?

OPHELIA: I didn't meet him. I found him.

BERGEN: You found him! Where?

OPHELIA: Under my bed. He was a—a—burglar.

[95]

BERGEN: Really? Oh, you poor, poor girl!

OPHELIA: It wasn't that bad, Mr. Bergen. He said, "If you scream, I'll kill you." Oh, he was wonderful!

BERGEN: You'd better keep your doors and windows locked, Ophelia. Then you won't have burglars.

OPHELIA: I know what I'm doing. I even put a bottle of beer under the bed every night. But he has never come back.

BERGEN: I see. Aren't you afraid, Ophelia, living alone?

OPHELIA: I'm not alone now. I have a dog— a watch dog. And he's trained, too.

BERGEN: Who trained him?

OPHELIA: I did. I trained him to bite every man.

BERGEN: You mean, if the man tries to break into the house.

OPHELIA: No. If he tries to leave the house.

BERGEN: I imagine that you were very popular, when you were a girl, Ophelia.

OPHELIA: Well—I didn't waste much time knitting, Mr. Bergen. In my day I was what you'd call a humdinger.

BERGEN: That's certainly interesting. Did you enjoy good health when you were young, Ophelia?

OPHELIA: No, Mr. Bergen. I enjoyed very bad health. I was a frail and delicate girl. I always fainted at just the right time. But I suffered a great deal. I suffered so much that I didn't feel well unless I was suffering. I didn't mind the suffering, though. It was just the pain I couldn't stand.

BERGEN: I see. Is your health better now, Ophelia?

OPHELIA: Yes, it is, Mr. Bergen. Much better. In fact, it is so good that I have taken up athletic sports.

BERGEN: Is that so? What are you doing?

OPHELIA: Fancy diving. I do a standing, sitting half-gainer and a one and a half jack-knife.

[97]

BERGEN: This is a surprise to me, Ophelia. I didn't know that you were a fancy diver.

OPHELIA: I'm a diving fool. And I'm a fool to dive. But the results are worth it, Mr. Bergen.

BERGEN: What results?

OPHELIA: The life guards, Mr. Bergen. The life guards. They always stand by with boat hooks to pull me out.

BERGEN: Then there's method in your madness.

OPHELIA: Yes, indeed. And madness in my methods. By the way, Mr. Bergen, if you're not busy tonight, would you like to come over to my house and look at my stereoscope pictures?

BERGEN: Thank you, Ophelia. I'll certainly try to be there. Shall I bring candy or flowers?

OPHELIA: Maybe you'd better bring hamburger for the dog, Mr. Bergen.

CHAPTER VI

Its name exactly describes "distant" ventriloquism. The success of this type of ventriloquial entertainment depends upon the ventriloquist's ability to produce the illusion of a voice coming from a distant place. Unlike "near" ventriloquism, "distant" ventriloquism requires no dummies or puppets. The ventriloquist indicates the position of the unseen speaker and the exact spot from which the voice is supposed to come, by an expressive gesture or by looking in that direction.

In popular language "distant" ventriloquism is often called "voice throwing." That is a very inaccurate name. As I explained in Chapter 1, the voice is not thrown. The illusion of distance is produced by the diffusion of the voice which, in turn, is created by pressure on the vocal cords. The pressure is decreased to give the effect of great distance. It is gradually increased if the unseen speaker is supposed to move nearer to the ventriloquist. The greater the pressure, the nearer the invisible speaker will seem to be.

The first steps in the study and practice of "distant" ventriloquism are the same as in the "near" type. You must learn to speak clearly and distinctly without moving your lips and to produce a natural-sounding ventriloquial voice. As in "near" ventriloquism, the "drone" is the foundation of all "distant" ventriloquial voices, the variation in pressure on the vocal cords indicating the degree of distance from which the voice is supposed to come. When you have succeeded in producing a clear "drone" and in

varying its tonal quality, when you have learned to speak without lip movement and when
you have mastered the smooth change from
your ventriloquial voice to your natural voice,
you have built a firm foundation for your success as a "distant" ventriloquist.

Before proceeding further in your practice of
"distant" ventriloquism, I suggest that you
make a careful study of the tonal qualities of
sounds and voices at different distances, in order to reproduce similar sounds correctly in your
ventriloquial voice. You will notice that a
sound becomes weaker as it grows more distant,
that its pitch remains the same regardless of
distance and that human voices become muffled, especially in the pronunciation of consonants, as they grow more distant, until they
gradually become completely obscured and in-
audible.

After this study, the next step is to learn the
different degrees of pressure necessary to pro-

duce these various distant sounds. In all cases, regardless of distance, touch the base of your tongue to your soft palate, forming a sort of diaphragm which allows only a very small part of the voice to pass, when speaking in your ventriloquial voice. Always remember to keep your lungs extended and to emit as little breath as possible. When you have mastered this phase of ventriloquial speaking, you are ready to practice the variation of pressure and the creating of the illusion of different distances.

I suggest that first you practice the imitation of a voice speaking from behind a closed door. Ask one of your friends to talk to you from behind a door. You will discover that his voice, while louder and more distinct than a more distant voice, has a hollow, muffled tone. That same tonal quality exists in a voice which comes from a box or trunk.

To produce this behind-the-door or inside-the-trunk voice, press the tongue against the

Distant ventriloquism requires no dummy

teeth, which must be set closely together. Part your lips slightly and fill your lungs with air, keeping your breath under complete control. Then speak in the ventriloquial "drone," muffling your words into a slightly indistinct hollowness.

To gain additional realism in using the closet or trunk voice, it is very effective to open the door of the closet or to lift the lid of the trunk occasionally. The movement must be accompanied by a corresponding change in the tone and strength of the ventriloquial voice. As the door is slowly opened, or the trunk lid lifted, the voice will become louder and the words more distinct until, when it is entirely open, the voice will be full and strong, although it will still retain its slightly hollow characteristics. To do this, allow the tones of your voice to roll forward from the back of your throat to the front part of your mouth, gradually increasing the pressure on your vocal cords. Your closed teeth and partly closed lips will create the hollow, muffled effect.

When the door is closed or the lid is dropped, the procedure is reversed, the voice gradually receding to the back of the throat and the pressure slowly decreasing.

To produce the voice which seems to come from above you, force your "drone" voice forward against the roof of your mouth and pitch the tone higher. The result will be a gruff falsetto voice, with a high pitch. Keep your jaws rigid and roll back your tongue, with your lips slightly parted, thus elevating your palate, drawing it nearer to the pharynx and forming a cavity in the back part of your mouth and throat. The voice produced under these conditions might be called an "explosive" voice, since the words will be "exploded" against the roof of your mouth by your sudden expulsions of breath from your lungs through the small cavity in the back of your throat.

When using this voice, you must pay careful attention to your breathing if you wish to obtain effective results. The breath must be allowed to escape very slowly from the lungs, thus subduing and muffling the tones and creating the illusion of distance. Also you must direct the attention of your audience upward by looking and pointing toward the ceiling. This will greatly enhance the illusion that an unseen person is speaking from the room above you or from the roof.

The voice, which seems to come from below you, is different in many ways from the behind-the-door voice or the voice-from-above. Its chief difference is in its tonal quality. Instead of being a muffled "drone" or a high-pitched falsetto, it is a guttural voice, produced as far down in the throat as possible.

In practicing this voice, shorten your neck until your chin touches your chest. This compresses the vocal cords and draws up your

Your acting ability is important

stomach in such a manner that, when you speak, the sound cannot rise but is forced downward in the throat. When you have practiced this voice until you can produce it with ease and clearness, it will not be necessary to lower your chin to your chest. You will find that you can speak in this guttural voice while standing in a normal position in front of your audience.

In other words, the three "distant" voices are produced by sending the sound in the direction from which you wish it to seem to come. The near-at-hand voice, supposedly coming from a trunk or from behind a closed door, is confined to the cavity of the mouth. The voice from above is produced by forcing the sound upward against the roof of the mouth. The voice from below is made by forcing the sound downward in the throat and pitching the tones to a guttural lowness.

After continued practice has made you expert in producing these voices, you can combine the three, bringing your unseen companion downstairs, taking him upstairs and opening and closing the door behind which he is standing. But I advise you to attempt this complicated type of ventriloquial entertainment only

after you have become expert in rolling your voice from the back of your throat to the roof of your mouth and in changing your ventriloquial voice from low, guttural tones to a high-pitched, explosive sound. I suggest that, in the beginning, you place your invisible companion in one spot and keep him there during your conversation.

Always remember, too, that your acting ability is very important in producing the effects which you desire. The movements of your eyes and body, when you speak in your natural voice to your unseen companion, will plainly indicate his supposed whereabouts. Your facial expression, when listening to the words of your invisible partner, will play a very important part in the dramatic and humorous realism of your entertainment. Since you have no dummy or puppet to share the attention of your audience, your gestures and facial expressions have a doubled importance. You must learn to be a good actor, as well as a good ventriloquist, when you are studying and practicing "distant" ventriloquism.

CHAPTER VII

ENTERTAINING WITH DISTANT VENTRILOQUISM

The great advantage which "distant" ventriloquism has for a beginner is that it requires no expensive accessories. You can stage an amusing and successful act without the use of dolls or puppets of any kind. However, because of the absence of these aids, your own acting ability is of even greater importance than it is in "near" ventriloquism. Of course, if you are not absolutely sure of yourself and your skill, it is possible to turn away from the audience when you are listening to the voice of your unseen companion, thus hiding your face and any telltale lip movement. But I do not advise you to do this, if you can avoid it, as it destroys a large part of the effectiveness of your act.

If you are entertaining in a room or a small hall, seat your audience as far away from you as possible. Prepare your dialogue with care, making a real human being of your invisible partner. When talking in your natural voice, speak with dramatic vigor and clearness of tone. This will accentuate the muffled, distant sound of your ventriloquial voice. Also, except in rare cases where your audience is far removed, place your self between your listeners and the place from which your ventriloquial voice is supposed to come.

As in the case of "near" ventriloquism entertainments, humor is the primary factor in successful acts. Although you have no visible puppet, you can create the illusion of an unseen human companion by designing your dialogue to fit a definite personality. I advise the beginner to create in his own mind one distinct,

An unseen third person makes a three-sided conversation possible

although unseen, personality and to concentrate on that one invisible companion, writing the dialogue to fit his imagined sex, age and general characteristics.

When you have progressed beyond the beginners' ranks, it is possible to stage a more elaborate entertainment, using both "near" and "distant" ventriloquism. For instance, you can carry on a three-sided conversation between yourself, a dummy seated on your knee and an unseen third person, supposedly hidden in a trunk, behind a closed door, in the room above you or in the cellar below you. However, I do not advise you to attempt this complicated type of entertainment unless you have become very skilled in both kinds of ventriloquism.

Always remember in "distant" ventriloquism, as well as in "near" ventriloquism, to maintain a rapid tempo in your dialogue. Don't hesitate or pause when changing from your natural to your ventriloquial voice. Keep up a brisk pace from the beginning to the end of your entertainment. That steady, smooth, swift flow of conversation is one of the secrets of a successful act.

The following is one of the dialogues which Charlie McCarthy and I used for a radio broadcast. It was originally designed, of course, for "near" ventriloquism, but I have changed it slightly to meet the requirements of "distant" ventriloquism. You can follow it as a model, if you wish, in writing your own "distant" ventriloquism dialogue.

During the following conversation I am standing either near a closed door or beside a stairway. Charlie's voice is supposed to come either from another room or from the floor above me.

* * * *

HOW TO BECOME A VENTRILOQUIST

EDGAR BERGEN: Charlie, where are you?

CHARLIE MCCARTHY: I'm in the library, Mr. Bergen.   (OR) I'm upstairs in my bedroom, Mr. Bergen.

BERGEN: What are you doing?

CHARLIE: I'm studying my lessons.

BERGEN: Well, I'm glad to hear that. How have you been doing with your school work?

CHARLIE: Very nicely—very nicely, indeed.

BERGEN: That's strange. I have a letter from a Mr. Ramshackle, saying that he is the truant officer in this district and that he has no record of your enrollment in any school. He also says that he has written you twice.

CHARLIE: Four times—to be exact.

BERGEN: Charlie, you don't mean to tell me that you have been skipping school!

CHARLIE: No—I didn't mean to tell you.

BERGEN: In New York you promised me that if I took you to California you would study hard.

CHARLIE: Well—that was back in New York. Believe me, Mr. Bergen, I've tried so hard to find a school. But I'm a stranger out here—all alone. Day after day I looked. But no matter what street car I got on, I always ended up at the beach.

BERGEN: You will pay for this folly, Charlie. You are a ship without anchor or port—a butterfly drifting aimlessly before the breeze.

CHARLIE: Please say no more. I can't stand it. I hate myself.

BERGEN: Have you ever thought of the future, Charlie?

CHARLIE: Yes, I have, Mr. Bergen. Only the other day I had a long talk with myself about the future. I spoke up. I didn't mince words.

BERGEN: What did you say?

CHARLIE: I said, "Charlie, old boy"—chummy like—"old boy Charlie"—I call myself by my first name. After all, why shouldn't I? It was an informal talk.

BERGEN: Yes, of course. But what did you say?

CHARLIE: I said, "Charlie, old boy, what's going to become of you?"

BERGEN: What was the answer?

CHARLIE: Well, sir, you know, I had myself cornered.

BERGEN: In these days of keen competition education is essential to success. Knowledge is the power that drives the vehicle of industry. Where do you fit, Charlie?

CHARLIE: I guess I'm just a trailer, Mr. Bergen.

BERGEN: With that attitude you can be positive of failure, young man.

CHARLIE: Well, it's nice to be sure about something.

BERGEN: Where will you be twenty years from now?

CHARLIE: I'll meet you there, wherever it is. For that matter, where would you be right now without me, Mr. Bergen? I say that experience and travel are great teachers. Study, alone, won't make you a big man.

BERGEN: There is truth in that, Charlie.

CHARLIE: I wouldn't trade some of my experiences for anything. Take, for example, the time I went grouse shooting in the Scottish uplands with Lord Thittersfield.

BERGEN: You mean, you were grouse shooting?

CHARLIE: Oh, definitely! I go every autumn. What fun!

BERGEN: Did you have any luck?

CHARLIE: Oh, definitely! Why, the first day out I got three cocker spaniels. The second day I got a horse and Lord Thittersfield. I don't miss a thing. If it moves, I shoot. If anyone shoots, I move.

BERGEN: I don't believe you were ever in Scotland and I don't believe you ever went grouse shooting, Charlie.

CHARLIE: Oh, come now, Mr. Bergen. Yes, I was—and yes, I did.

Charlie talking from his room upstairs

BERGEN: I don't believe you.

CHARLIE: You don't? Well, anyway, I tried.

BERGEN: Come here, Charlie. I want to talk to you seriously.

CHARLIE: And I want to talk to you, too, Mr. Bergen. But not seriously. I'd like to say a word or two about that baseball game tomorrow.

BERGEN: We'll talk about your education—not about baseball—young man. Come here.

CHARLIE: Maybe, since we're on the subject of education, I'd better finish my lessons first.

BERGEN: You can finish your lessons later. I want to talk to you now.

CHARLIE: Very well. But remember, Mr. Bergen, it's you who are tearing me away from my education. It's you who are making me a trailer, instead of an engine.

BERGEN: Don't be ridiculous, Charlie! Are you coming or are you not?

CHARLIE: I'm on my way, Mr. Bergen. So help me, I am.